10 Ways to Become Debt Free

...Tips to help you Gain Financial Freedom

Proven resources to get assistance with paying student loans, past due hospital bills, a plan to show you how to eliminate credit card debt and more.

By Yolanda Washington-Cowan

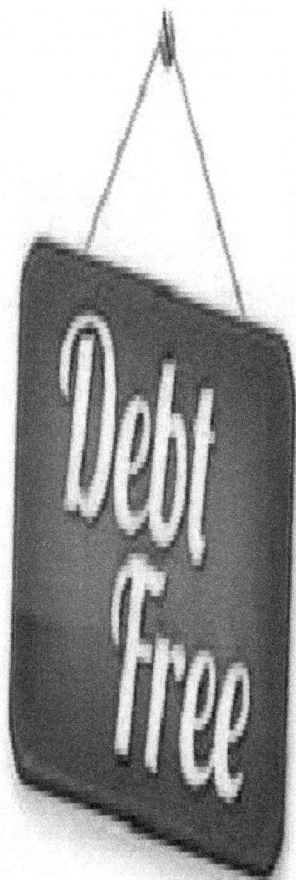

Copyright © 2018
10 Ways to Become Debt Free
...Tips to help you Gain Financial Freedom
By Yolanda Washington Cowan

ISBN: 13: 978-0-9997776-4-0
ISBN-10: 0-9997776-4-5
Published by
B-Inspired Publishing
7285 Winchester Road, Suite 109
Memphis, TN 38125
www.B-Inspiredpub.com
Printed in the United States
First Edition: July 2018

Table of Contents

Introduction

Many of us find ourselves standing on a precipice over the chasm of debt, hanging on by our toenails. The majority of people in the United States are in debt. More and more people are taking their debt into retirement. While a chunk of the population has a mortgage as part of that debt, a growing percentage of the population have replaced mortgage debt with student loans, car loans, and credit card loans as their top debts.

There are so many living from paycheck to paycheck. That is stressful enough if you can keep it up, but if you hit even the smallest bump in the road (an illness, a family emergency, natural disaster, accident, etc.), you can start going under fast! While a manageable debt isn't necessarily a problem, debt that you can't afford can leave you feeling as if you're drowning.

You can't afford to ignore your debt; it won't go away on its own. This book is meant to be a life-preserver for those who need it. If you read and apply some of the ideas in this book like budgeting, prioritizing, cutting out credit cards, negotiating with creditors, etc., it can help you not just keep your head above water, but swim strong and steadily until you get to a debt-free shore.

CHAPTER 1
PLAN AND CREATE A BUDGET

The average American spends $1.25 for every $1 that they make! If that's the case, it's no wonder that most of us have such a problem with debt. Many of us go blithely through our week or month spending our money with little planning. We get what we think we need or want and pay bills with what is left over, giving little thought to the future. That may work for a while, but what happens if there is an unexpected medical issue or if you lose your job? What if your car gives up the ghost? If you're living paycheck to paycheck without creating any kind of safety net, you could be in for some serious drama.

One way to avoid some of that drama is to create a budget. Now, hold on, 'budget' doesn't have to be a dirty word. Instead of seeing it as a buzzkill, look at your budget as something that allows you to reach your goals. If you save a little now, you can buy that (fill in the blank) later without going into debt for it. As a matter of fact, if you can do it, did you know that saving the equivalent of a house payment each month for ten yrs. will allow you to pay cash for a house instead of going into debt for it? You can get there even quicker if you put that money into a savings account where it earns interest for you. Most people literally pay three times as much for a house than the actual cost of the house because they are paying interest on a loan! That's why what could take them ten years, takes them 30 years instead. Here are some tips for laying out a budget that works for you.

1. Make a list of what you own and what you owe.

2. Figure out how much money you make each month.

3. Never spend more money than what you have. Don't use a credit card to pay for day to day living expenses.

Keeping good records can make a huge difference in getting out of debt. You need to know what you have available and what you have going out. It may not be fun, but it really is essential in keeping on top of your finances. If you don't, you'll get to the end of the month and wonder where all your money went. By documenting your spending, you'll be able to see where you made any budget mistakes and you can try to correct that in the following month.

For most people, determining what they make each month is pretty simple, but for some, it can be a little trickier. Some people don't make a set amount each week. For some, their income fluctuates depending on the number of hours they work; some weeks they may see more hours, some weeks fewer. If your income varies from one week to the next, watch the trends and try to find an average income for you.

Number two sounds like a no-brainer, but you'd be surprised at how many of us spend what we don't have. How many of you can remember playing the game of figuring out just how long it would take that check to clear? Now that everything's gone digital, the person at the checkout knows immediately if you have enough in your account to cover that purchase. Sometimes we do it by spending before we've taken out the money that should be used to pay our bills.

If you are using credit cards to meet your daily needs, then something needs to change. You are not only living well beyond your means; you are only digging yourself deeper and deeper into debt. The problem may stem from not understanding the difference between needs and wants.

Needs are pretty universal for each human being. Things like food, clothing, and shelter meet the definition of needs. Wants go a little deeper into those things. For instance, we all need food, but we don't *need* the choicest cuts of meat or that decadent chocolate cake. We don't need designer clothing either, or a mansion; those are *wants*.

Your food budget is actually a good place to start if you're looking for an area to cut back. Pricey snack foods can be cut almost without you noticing their absence. Cutting coupons and following in-store specials can save you more than you might think. Planning your weekly menu based on what's on special this week can free up funds for other areas. Just make sure that you don't get sucked into buying things you won't use just because they're on sale.

Get a system for paying your bills. Whether you use the envelope strategy, automatic online funds transfer, or some other system, you need to have a workable plan. Late fees add up quickly and are totally unnecessary if you plan ahead.

Another thing to budget for that people often forget is home upkeep. It's important to be good stewards of what you have. If you don't pay attention to upkeep now, you could be in for some big home repair bills later. Do a walk-around home inspection in both the spring and the fall. Check your siding and windowsills. Have a look at masonry and your foundation. Little cracks can lead to big damage. Have your roof inspected every year. Catching wear and tear or storm damage early can save you money in the long run. Think about the 'big-ticket' items that may need replacing in the next twenty years or so, things like replacing your roof, a new water heater, kitchen appliances, air conditioning, furnace, etc. When budgeting for these things, don't forget to figure in the cost of labor and installation.

Remember, if you don't plan now, you could suffer for it in the future. Although you may dream of retiring someplace warm and sunny, many older Americans have a hard time paying for basic needs. The average American spends $1.25 for every $1 that they make! If that's the case, it's no wonder that most of us have such a problem with debt.

Getting out of debt doesn't just happen; it has to be intentional. Theirs is a Scripture in Proverbs that says, "Good planning and hard work lead to prosperity." It takes discipline and stick-to-itiveness. It isn't easy, but we all know that it's what's right.

Sample Monthly Budget Planning Worksheet

Month of:	Amount	Due Date		Amount	Due Date
MONTHLY INCOME			**LIVING & HEALTH**		
Salary			Grocery		
Tips			Restaurants		
Bonus/Dividends			Entertainment/Dates		
Miscellaneous			Salon/Hair		
FIRST FRUITS			Toiletries/Makeup		
Tithe/Giving			Clothing		
Savings			Health Insurance		
Buffer			Daycare/Babysitter		
HOME			Pets (Food/Vet/Grooming)		
Mortgage/Rent			Personal Money (Hers)		
Taxes/Insurance			Personal Money (His)		
Association Fees			**DEBT**		
Maintenance/Repairs			Cay Payment 1		
Household Goods			Car Payment 2		
UTILITIES			Credit Card 1		
Electric			Credit Card 2		
Water/Sewer/Trash			Credit Card 3		
Gas/Oil			School Loan 1		
Cable			School Loan 2		
Internet			Other		
Phone			Other		
TRANSPORTATION			**BUDGET TOTALS**		
Insurance			Total Monthly Income	$0	
Gasoline			Total Monthly Expenses	$0	
Maintenance/Repairs			Amount Remaining	$0	

Monthly Household Budget

Expenses	Budgeted	Spent	Difference
HOUSING			
Mortgage/Rent	$	$	$
Property Taxes	$	$	$
Insurance	$	$	$
Other	$	$	$
UTILITIES			
Electricity	$	$	$
Gas	$	$	$
Water/Sewer	$	$	$
Home Phone	$	$	$
Cell Phone	$	$	$
Internet	$	$	$
Cable	$	$	$
DEBT PAYMENTS			
Car Loan	$	$	$
Student Loan	$	$	$
Credit Cards	$	$	$

Income

Source	Amount
Wages	$
Wages	$
Child Support	$
Alimony	$
Benefits	$
Bonus/Tips	$
Other	$
Total	$

Budget Notes

CHAPTER 2
USE THE DEBT SNOWBALL PLAN
TO GET OUT OF DEBT

The first thing to consider is what kind of debt you have. There is 'good debt' and 'bad debt.' Good debt is money that you've borrowed for a home or education. These debts can be tax deductible and can also help to bolster your financial position. Bad debt usually takes the form of a credit card loan or a personal bank loan. These are the types of loans that you can't pay off in full in a couple of months. They also do nothing to boost your financial position. As long as you are making regular installment payments on your 'good debts,' you don't need to put extra pressure on yourself to pay them off quickly. So, your focus should be on those 'bad debts.'

Some places will tell you that you should start with the debt with the highest interest rate and pay that off first. While that sounds good in theory, it isn't always the best practice. Paying off the highest interest rate first may get you out of debt faster by a small margin, but sometimes a better idea is to get rid of the smallest debt first and then roll that money into the paying off the next debt and so on. This is especially true if you feel overwhelmed by the sheer number of bills you get each month that are trying to collect on a debt.

Your first step should be to get caught up on all of your bills and have $1,000 in savings, that way you won't be relying on your credit card accounts for your emergency funding. That savings won't happen all at once. The trick is to save 10% of each paycheck right off of the top before you spend any of it. The old saying, 'you can't miss what you haven't had' applies here. If possible, have the money deposited directly into your savings each week. This emergency fund can be a real lifesaver for those unexpected times.

Once you have your bills current and the $1,000 savings in place, you are ready to start on the debt snowball approach. Why is this a better idea than paying off the debt with the highest interest rate first? It keeps you motivated. Psychologically, if you have two debts, it feels like more than if you have one; even if the amount you owe is the same. Think about it this way, if you owe two debts, one for $60 and one for $40, it feels like you owe more than if you owe one debt for $100. You feel better if you pay off that $40 debt and then tackle the $60 debt than if you are slowly chipping away at the $100 debt, even if you are paying them off at the same rate. If you are paying off your smaller debts, it's easier to see your progress. The positive feedback that you get from paying off those little debts can make such a profound impact on you, that your commitment to staying on track with your debt repayment plan will be strengthened and you will have a better chance of success.

We could all use a little positive reinforcement now and then. Who doesn't like being told they're doing a good job? It's just the way we're wired. Paying off the debt with the highest interest rate might make sense on paper, but if you don't feel as if you're making inroads fast enough, you might give up before you have a chance to make a difference. Your most important goal is to get out of debt, with that in mind, you've got to go with what keeps you motivated.

Here's how to get started:

1. **Make a list and check it twice.** Sit down and make a list of all of your debts starting from the bottom (the lowest amount owed) and working your way up to the biggest (the greatest amount owed).

2. **Pay what you have to, and then pay some more.** Make the bare bones minimum payments on each one, *except* the lowest debt that you owe. Pay as much as you can possibly spare on the smallest debt. When you have that small debt paid off, take whatever you were paying on that and add it to what you are paying on the next one up on the list while continuing the minimum payments on the others.

3. **Keep going.** It's like in those old Saturday morning cartoons with Bugs and Daffy. The snowball picks up more snow, getting bigger and bigger as it rolls downhill. The more debts you pay off, the more money you'll have freed up to go toward the next one. Just make sure that you don't use that 'free money' to go out and accumulate new debt! That would be like taking one step forward and two steps back. Please, don't stop keep that momentum going!

Just a tiny pebble starts off at the top of a snowy hill and rolls down the embankment picking up more and more snow as it goes, getting bigger and more intimidating, that money that you freed up and added to your payments grows. Soon, what had been a tiny pebble has turned into a massive snowball that threatens to wipe out the chalet at the foot of the mountain. Think how great it would feel when your snowball wipes out your debt! So, keep going. Don't give up. Revel in the feeling you get when you see those debts disappearing one by one!

Debt Snowball Example

DEBT SNOWBALL

Your Debt	Total Payoff	Minimum Payment	New Payment
Private Student Loan	$2,500	$25	$25
Khols Credit Card	$3,000	$15	$40
Federal Student Loan	$4,000	$20	$60

Debt Snowball Notes

_____

_____

_____

_____

_____

_____

_____

_____

_____

_____

_____

_____

_____

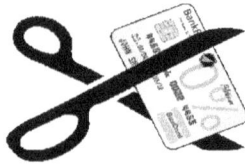

CHAPTER 3
STOP USING CREDIT CARDS

Credit cards are convenient. Credit cards offer rewards. If you're already drowning in debt, however, and credit cards have already caused you problems, then you should avoid them like the plague! Using tomorrow's money to pay for today's bills is a recipe for disaster. If you don't have enough money to pay off your credit card completely each month, you shouldn't use it. You know that, but you've gotten into the cycle of paying for everything from bills to impulse buys with that little piece of plastic. Now you want to stop, but you don't really know how.

1. **Create that emergency fund.** If you find yourself using your credit card for minor emergencies, then you know that you've got a problem. Here's where that emergency fund can come in handy. This will help you to slowly get away from your dependency on your credit cards.

2. **Put them away.** Not just away in your wallet but put them somewhere that is inconvenient. Put them in a filing cabinet, put them in the bottom of your dresser, heck, you can even freeze them in a block of ice in your freezer.

Talk about frozen assets! The point is to put them somewhere that will take some real effort to get to them and use them. That will help you to think twice and avoid those impulse purchases.

3. **Close your account.** Closing your credit card account is pretty simple. It usually only takes one phone call. Closing a credit card account can have a temporarily negative impact on your credit score, but if that's what you need to do to avoid going deeper into debt, do it. A temporary hitch in your credit is better than digging yourself deeper into debt.

4. **Shred it.** Did you know that the office paper shredder will work on a credit card too? Yep, and if your card is reduced to nothing more than strips of plastic, you can't use it. Just make sure that the credit card number is unreadable so that your identity can't be stolen. You may even want to dispose of the strips in several different trashes so that thieves won't be able to play jigsaw with the pieces later on.

5. **Do leave home without it.** Window shopping can be just that if you leave your credit card at home. Buyer's remorse will drop dramatically if you stop those impulse buys before they start. If you find something that you actually

need, you can always come back for it once you have the cash. Sometimes the trip home and back can give you time to reconsider your purchases. You may decide that it's something you can do without after all.

6. **Reality check.** Do you know how much you spend on interest every year? How about how long it will take you to pay off the balance on your card? The answers may shock you. If you owe $1,000 and have a 14% interest rate on that card, you're looking at 4 ½ years to pay it off if you're making the minimum $25 payments per month. Doing it that way also means that by the end of that time, you'll have paid $347.55 in interest alone. Look at your credit card statement and see just how much you've paid in interest so far this year. The answer may just be the dose of reality you need to make you put down those cards for good.

7. **A spoonful of sugar helps the medicine go down.** Sometimes it's nice to give yourself a little treat, especially if you've done a good job. For every week that you refrain from using your credit card, treat yourself to something inexpensive that you wouldn't normally get just for you. The key here is to remember the term 'inexpensive.' You don't want to undo all your hard work by blowing it on a treat.

8. **Consolidate your credit card balances onto one or two cards.** Sit down with your most recent credit card statements. See which ones have the lowest interest rates, then you can consolidate your balances onto these credit cards. If you get in touch with credit card company, you can give them the information for the other cards and they can initiate a balance transfer. Be sure to ask for a transfer fee waiver. If they won't agree to waive the fee, you may want to consider using one of your other credit card accounts instead.

9. **Consider an unsecured personal loan.** You might see if you can get an unsecured personal loan to consolidate your balances. With a loan like this, you can end up with a lower interest rate and have the ability to pay off your credit card debts quicker. Once those credit card accounts are paid off, you can close those accounts.

10. **Just say no.** Self-control is almost a lost art in our society today. We want what we want when we want it. Discipline and self-control seem like skills that not many people possess, whether it's resisting that second helping of pie or those pretty pumps we found on our favorite shopping site, sometimes it feels impossible. Do whatever it takes to reinforce the

notion that you shouldn't buy that. Whether it's reminding yourself of your dire financial straits or keeping a picture of the goal that you're working toward, do what is needed to resist the urge to use that card.

It isn't impossible to stop using credit cards. It can be done. Your first goal is to pay off the balance on your card account. Remember the adage out of sight out of mind? Well, that's a good one to apply here. If you don't see the money, you'll forget it's there. Arrange to have your payments automatically withdrawn from your bank account and make sure that you pay a little more than the minimum payment. That way you won't be tempted to let those payments slide. If you're paying off your balance and not adding to it, you'll be able to get away from credit cards for good.

Credit Card Debt Tracker Worksheet

credit card debt

Account: _____

DATE	OWE	PAID	BALANCE

CHAPTER 4
NEGOTIATE YOUR
PAYMENT WITH CREDITORS

Sometimes we get in over our heads. It can happen fast. An unexpected hospital stay can mean not only hospital bills, but lost wages too. Cutbacks at work can affect the best of us. We can be living high off the hog one day and be stuck envying the slop the hogs are fed the next. No matter how it happens, your best bet is to stop avoiding your creditors. Most creditors will be willing to negotiate with you.

Collectors often buy debts for much less than their face value. That's good news for you because they can accept less than full payment and still make a profit. Creditors may also be willing to strike a deal with you. It's better than writing off the debt as a loss.

Here are some tips that can help you negotiate with your creditors and the debt collectors.

- **That's my story, and I'm stickin' to it.** When you're on the phone with someone trying to explain your situation, they don't need your whole life story, but it if there is a legitimate reason that you have fallen behind, let them know. Don't change your story with each phone call, be consistent. They also need to hear what you are doing to get things moving in the right direction again.

- o For instance: I was in a car accident and off work for a couple of months. I'm trying to get things caught up.
- o I lost my job, and my new job is a big cut in pay. I'm trying to pick up more hours to help out.
- o Our son has been diagnosed with a serious illness, and my wife quit her job so that she could stay home with him. We're still adjusting to our new normal, but we're looking for ways to make cuts in our budget and get back to making regular payments.

- **Don't be melodramatic.** It's a sad truth, but some collectors act like bullies. If they can get to you, they may be able get you to promise more than you can comfortably do. They don't care who else gets gypped as long as it's not them. Don't let them make you lose your cool. If you have a problem, ask to speak with their supervisor. If that doesn't work, tell them that you will have to call them back. If you have to talk with that same representative later, let them know that you are recording your conversation. Sometimes that's enough to keep them from crossing the line.

- **When in doubt, ask.** A collector may try to tell you that you'll be sued or lose your property if you don't pay up. If that happens, keep calm and ask questions like, 'When will I get notice of this lawsuit?' Or 'When will that money come out of my account?' Sometimes the threats are just that, threats. Some of them may not even be legal. You may be ahead to call their bluff.

- **Write it down.** Have a tablet and pen beside your phone just for this specific purpose. When you talk with your creditors and the collectors, take notes. One of the first things that they tell you when they call is their name. If you didn't catch it the first time, ask them to repeat it and spell it if need be. Write down the day and time of your conversation and what you talk about. This helps you and keeps them honest as well.

- **Open, read, and save your mail.** Sometimes we think if we ignore something, it will go away. Wrong. Although it may be scary to open those collection letters, ignoring them will only make the situation worse. You need to open and read all of your mail, then save it in a safe place.

- **Get real.** By now, you've likely looked at your income and bills. See where you can cut back and figure out how much you can afford to pay to each creditor. Often you will get a better deal by agreeing to pay a one-time lump sum. Should you decide to go the route of a payment plan, make sure, you know the entire amount that you will need to pay when all is said and done.

- **Pay before it goes to collections.** You're better off dealing with creditors rather than a collections agency. An account that has been turned over to collections has a worse effect on your credit score than late payments do. Do your best to work something out with your creditors before it's too late.

- **Document it.** If you don't have something in writing, the terms can change without your consent. To avoid the he said, she said, get it in writing.

- **Get help.** A credit counseling agency can help you work with your creditors to come up with a payment plan that works for you. If it looks like you won't be able to pay off your debts, you can request a free consultation with a bankruptcy attorney. You may decide to file, you may decide not to, but the attorney can let you know just how far a creditor can go in their effort to collect.

- **Start with a clean slate.** If at all possible, get the creditor to agree to remove late payments from your record. Late payments, charge-offs, and collection accounts can all remain on your credit report for up to 7 years or more.

Remember, while agreeing to a debt settlement can be detrimental to your credit score, it's better than letting your debt wind up in a collections agency, or worse yet a judgment that could lead to garnishment of your wages or assets. Don't bury your head in the sand. Take charge of your debt; don't let it take charge of you.

Negotiation Notes

CHAPTER 5
START CUTTING COST –
DOWNSIZING

Downsizing doesn't have to mean living in a 'tiny house,' but it can mean that you go with something with fewer square feet and a smaller mortgage payment each month. You may not even need to sacrifice the square feet if you simply move to a more affordable area. You'd be surprised how much of a difference a good school district can make to the price of a home. If you don't have school-aged children to consider, looking at homes in an area with a less than stellar school district could save you some serious change. Downsizing can not only save you money on your mortgage; you can use the money you've freed up to pay off some of your other debts, like credit cards or student loans.

There are two steps involved in downsizing your home. First, you have to sell your current home, and second, you will need to buy one that is more affordable for you. That can be a big adjustment for you and your family. You'll need to make sure that you are prepared for the changes that will come your way.

The first thing you will need to consider is your current credit score. If you are looking to downsize, it's likely that you will need to secure a mortgage for another home before you've managed to sell your current home. If you're already in debt and looking to get out by downsizing, then your credit score probably isn't good enough to allow you to go this route.

Another option is to sell your current home first. This alternative is especially attractive if you have some equity in your current home. It will give you some cash in hand when you go to buy your new, downsized home. Depending on how much equity you have, you'll either have the money to buy your new home outright or make a decent down payment on a potential residence. Either way, it's wise to talk to a financial advisor before taking this step.

Many homeowners get an unwelcome surprise when they have their home appraised. They realize that they owe more on their home than what is worth. If this is the instance in your case, then you might want to see if your lender will commit to a short sale. A short sale is where you are not responsible for the difference between the selling price and the mortgage balance. Although the lender won't be getting the full amount they are owed, they will be better off with a short sale than with a foreclosure. In a foreclosure, a lender will lose approximately 50% while a short sale sees them losing only 30%.

Start by making a to-do list and have a definite timetable for finishing each step.

1. **Do some figuring.** You'll need to figure out how much you will save if you downsize your home.

2. **Find a real estate agent you can trust.** Talk with the agent and let them know how much you can afford to spend on your next home. Then ask them to sit down with you and explain what your buying options are.

3. **Look for understanding lenders.** Let potential lender know that you are looking to downsize. If they know that upfront, they may be more willing to work with you.

4. **DIY.** Your end goal is to get as much equity from your current home as you can. With this in mind, you should do your utmost to make sure that everything is in tip-top shape.

Downsizing your home can be freeing. It can feel as if the weight of the world is lifted off of your shoulders. You'll have less clutter to deal with and be better off financially. It can help you to be debt free and better prepared for the road ahead.

Downsizing Notes

CHAPTER 6
USE RESOURCES TO HELP
PAY PAST/OVERDUE
HOSPITAL BILLS

We all know that health insurance is a good thing. Unfortunately, it usually doesn't cover 100% of the costs when you're in the hospital. This can leave you on the hook for a fair chunk of change. There are some options available to help you out. First, go to the Health Resources and Services Administration website and see if the hospital where you were is covered under the Hill-Burton Act. If the facility received money from the government, they must offer free or reduced care to patients. The program has not received funding since 1997, but if you fall below the poverty guidelines, they are still under obligation to help you. Let's check out some of the other options out there.

1. **Government help-** At benefits.gov you can check to see if there are any benefits for which you may be eligible. There is a short questionnaire that can help you narrow down the benefits that best apply to you.
    - Make sure that you have your income information ready, as well as infor-

mation on any benefits you receive already. There are several pages, but at any point in the process, you can check for benefits results. The more information you provide, though, the better your chances of finding everything to which you may be entitled.

2. **State-sponsored programs-** Each state has its own programs geared toward providing assistance with medical care, prescription assistance, health insurance, medical supplies and equipment, disease screening, respite care, etc. To begin your search go to NeedyMeds.org, this will give you information about what you can find in your state.

3. **The United Way-** The United Way is well established in most communities, and you can get information about what type of medical assistance is available in your area by talking to a referral specialist. Just dial 211 or go to 221.org, they will be able to provide you with information on things ranging from alcohol and drug treatment to community clinics. They can also direct you toward senior services in your area.

4. **Children and Youth with Special Health Care Needs (CYSHCN)-** Having a child with disabilities can be expensive. Often there are extensive health care needs associated with disabilities. You may qualify for health care assistance through Children and Youth with Special Health Care Needs (CYSHCN). A child must have special needs to be eligible. The needs must be long-lasting and serious, including behavioral, physical, and emotional issues. Eligibility is income based, and your child's health condition and age do come into consideration, as well as the state in which you live. Some of the services offered are early intervention and screening for health risks, assistive technology, and family support. Go to FamilyVoices.org and click on the map for your state to find out more information about what your state offers. You may also contact your state's Department of Health & Human Services to find out more.

5. **CancerCare-** CancerCare is an organization which provides help to eligible families so that they can pay for the costs related to cancer treatment. If you meet the financial guideline limits and have a confirmed diagnosis of cancer for which you're are currently receiving treatment, you may qualify for assistance from their organization. CancerCare will help with

the cost of transportation, medical equipment, home care, child care, and medication costs. The help offered varies on the type of cancer that you have. For more information, call 1-800-813-HOPE (4673).

6. **Good Days from CDF-** Good Days from CDF can help you to pay for certain medications for such things as rheumatoid arthritis, multiple sclerosis, and Crohn's disease. This organization offers help for over 30 illnesses. It is required that you have health insurance before you receive assistance from them in addition to meeting certain income requirements.

7. **National Organization for Rare Disorders-** The National Organization for Rare Disorders (NORD) will help those with certain diseases which are covered by NORD by extending financial help to pay insurance premiums and copays, travel to disease specialists which are not covered by insurance, and diagnostic testing expenses. For those participating in clinical trials for some rare diseases, NORD works with other companies and organizations to arrange lodging and travel assistance.

8. **HealthWell Foundation-** The HealthWell Foundation provides assistance to patients dealing with chronic illnesses. The organization offers

help with health insurance premiums, deduct-ibles, and drug co-pays. There are several dis-eases covered under the umbrella of this foun-dation, everything from melanoma to gout. Funds are added throughout the year, so if you don't see your disease listed right away, check back later on, it may have been put on the list. Apply online or call 1-800-675-8416.

9. **Patient Advocate Foundation-** The Patient Advocate Foundation helps patients with such diseases as ovarian cancer, osteoporosis, and hepatitis B and C to pay for medication and to negotiate matters related to medical debt and copay assistance. To apply, you will need to have your Social Security number, insurance information and policy number, and combined household income.

10. **Crowdfunding-** GiveForward.com and Go-FundMe.com are two of the sites that have sprung up in recent years where people at-tempt to get others to donate money towards a specific goal like transplant surgery, service animals, or cancer treatment.

11. **Medical bill advocates-** If you're like most, you find that medical bills are complicated docu-ments and many can contain incorrect charg-es. Unless you are a medical professional, you

probably have a difficult time translating them. A medical bill advocate is a company or an individual who will go over your bill for a fee to make sure that everything is correct and you aren't being charged too much. Some will take a percentage of what money they save you, others charge by the hour. If you want to try to decipher your bill yourself, ask them for an EOB (explanation of benefits) or itemized bill. Things to look for include procedures listed incorrectly and duplicate charges.

- You should also make sure that, if you have insurance, you are not being charged for more than your insurance company has negotiated with your healthcare provider. If you check with your insurance company, you may find out that you are not on the hook for the difference.

12. **Haggle-** You never know unless you try, your doctor's office or hospital may be willing to take a lower amount than was originally listed. Your doctor may even be amenable to calling the hospital on your behalf. In most instances, they would rather work out some sort of payment plan than turn your case over for collections.

Unexpected hospital bills can be some of the most expensive bills you find yourself facing, but there is help. So, don't give up. Look into some of these options today.

Resource Notes

_____

_____

_____

_____

_____

_____

_____

_____

_____

_____

_____

_____

_____

CHAPTER 7
PAYING OFF STUDENT
LOANS

The average American household with student loan debt owes almost $50,000! That's second only to their mortgage debt. For many, this debt can be incredibly overwhelming. Thankfully, there are ways to pay off student loans.

1. **Put your assets to work-** There are many ways to use your own assets to help you pay off debt, including your student loans.

2. **Iraq-Afghanistan Service Grant-** If your parent died as a result of their military service in Iraq or Afghanistan, you might be eligible to receive over $5,000 to apply toward your student loans.

3. **National Health Service Corps Loan Repayment Program-** If you are a healthcare worker, you can get up to $50,000 in grants to help you pay off your student loans. In exchange, you will be required to work in a National Health Services Corps-approved site.

4. **John R. Justice Student Loan Repayment Program-** If you work in the legal profession as a state public defender or a state prosecutor, you may qualify for the John R. Justice Student Loan Repayment Program. This program can get you $10,000 a year for six years toward your student loans.

5. **National Institute of Mental Health Loan Repayment Program-** This grant can be for up to $35,000 toward medical school, graduate, or undergraduate debt. It is geared toward individuals who are in the healthcare profession and wish to pursue a career in social, behavioral, or clinical research at a non-profit organization.

6. **North Dakota Science, Technology, Engineering, and Mathematics (STEM) Student Loan Grant-** For those working in the fields of science, technology, engineering, and mathematics in the state of North Dakota, this grant is available to pay off their student loan debt.

7. **New York State Young Farmers Loan Forgiveness Incentive Program-** In New York state, those graduates who are interested in a farming career can get up to $10,000 a year for up to five years toward alleviating their student loan debts. Their degree must have come

from a New York university or college, and they must agree to farm in the state of New York for at least five years.

8. **Pennsylvania Primary Healthcare Loan Repayment Program-** If you are agreeable to get a job in the under-served portions of Pennsylvania as a physician or dentist, you may be eligible to receive anywhere from $30,000 to $100,000 toward student loans. A two-year service commitment is required.

9. **Nurse Corps Repayment Program-** The Nurse Corps Repayment Program through the Health Resources and Services Administration offers money to nurses to pay off up to 85% of their loans. To qualify, you must be a nurse practitioner, a registered nurse, or a nursing faculty member with a nursing degree. To apply, you must also work at either an accredited school of nursing or a healthcare facility.

10. **Teacher Cancellation-** For those who have taken out Federal Perkins Loans, you may be eligible for up to 100% loan forgiveness in exchange for teaching service. The loan will be canceled in increments including the interest that was accumulated throughout the year. To qualify, you must be a full-time teacher for a full academic year in one of these situations:

- a special education teacher
- in a school which serves students from low-income families
- a teacher in the fields of science, mathematics, foreign languages, or any area which the state education agency has determined has a shortage.

You may not fall under any of these categories. That doesn't mean that you should give up hope. There are still options out there available to you.

1. **Income-driven repayment plans-** If you have federal loans and are still having a difficult time meeting your payments, income-driven repayment plans might be the answer. Here are the four different plans:

   Income-Contingent Repayment
   - Income-Based Repayment
   - Pay as You Earn
   - Revised Pay as You Earn

While each plan is slightly different, they all follow the same basic principle. The government will look at your income and determine how much you need to pay each month. This can reduce how much you owe each month, which can give you a little breathing room.

2. **Public Service Loan Forgiveness-** If you were ineligible for student loan grants, but you work for a non-profit or for the government, you

might be eligible for Public Service Loan For-giveness. Under the terms of this arrangement, you must work for ten years while making the qualifying payments on your federal student loans; then the government will waive the re-maining balance. The forgiven balance is not taxable as income.

3. **Refinancing your loans-** If the above options don't work for you, you might want to consider refinancing your loans. This can get you a lower interest rate, or a lower monthly pay-ment. This is another way to save money in the long haul or simply allow you to manage your current budget a little easier.

Finally, if you're willing to give back to your community and those around the world, you could qualify for some of these opportunities:

4. **AmeriCorps-** AmeriCorps is an organization that allows you to gain some real-life work and educational experiences while offering your time to national service work. You will work in a service position that is geared toward your interests, skills, or preferred location, helping out in communities from coast to coast. The service is from 10 months to a year. Most of the opportunities are full-time. However, there are a few part-time positions available. The majority of AmeriCorps members will be eligi-

ble for postponement or forbearance of their loan repayment during the course of their service. Once your service is finished, you will be given a Segal AmeriCorps Education Award to put toward payment of your college, vocational training, graduate school, or repayment of student loans. The amount of the award varies from year to year as it is tied to the U.S. Department of Education's Pell Grant. You will also receive a small living allowance that would cover your daily needs. Some programs also provide housing and health insurance.

- **The Peace Corps-** Americans are sent throughout the world to help those in most urgent need. Peace Corps volunteers not only meet the immediate needs of those they serve, but they help to ensure that the change will last long after they leave. The work that you would do would depend on what is needed and what your skills are. Some of the skills needed fall under these headings:

  - Youth in Development
  - Education
  - Health
  - Agriculture
  - Community Economic Development

- HIV/AIDS
- Environment
- Earth Day
- Food Security
- Stomp Out Malaria

A term of service is usually two years. Public student loans may qualify for a deferment. Four Years of service may qualify you for up to 70% of loan forgiveness while a readjustment allowance of $7,425 is available once service is complete. It's a good idea to consult a financial aid advisor about the types of loans that you have, as the regulations surrounding each loan is a little different.

As a Peace Corps volunteer, you will earn a monthly allowance to cover your living and housing expenses, full medical and dental coverage, paid travel expenses, and 48 days of paid vacation.

Don't let student loan debt get you down. Paying off your student loan debt isn't impossible. With a little research becoming debt free is attainable.

Student Loan Notes

_____

_____

_____

_____

_____

_____

_____

_____

_____

_____

_____

_____

_____

_____

CHAPTER 8
REVAMP YOUR DATE-NIGHT PLANS TO CUT COST BUT STILL MAKE IT ENJOYABLE

Date-night doesn't have to be expensive. With a little planning, you and your partner can have date-nights that are fun without breaking the bank. One of the things to be sure that you have nailed down ahead of time is your childcare. If you plan things right, you can get free childcare by making your date-night plans coincide with your children's sleep-overs at their friend's or grandparent's house. Looking for some cost-effective ideas for your next date-night? Here are a few!

- **Take advantage of local trails-** Urban trails have sprouted up in communities across the country. Taking advantage of these trails can be a fun way to spend some quality time together with zero cost. Whether you bike or hike the trails is totally up to you. Do whatever you both enjoy. Give yourselves plenty of time to enjoy the scenery. Many of these trails have picnic areas near the parking areas, so you could pack a cooler with a picnic to eat either before or after your trek along the trails, saving you even more.

- **Go bowling-** A couple of games of bowling usually doesn't cost much, and a little friendly competition can spice up your relationship!

- **Go dancing-** Ballroom dancing has had resurgence in popularity recently thanks to some popular prime-time shows. If you check, you can probably find a studio near you. Introductory classes usually aren't that expensive.

- **Volunteer together-** Your time together doesn't have to be just about you. Giving back to the community in one way or the other can bring you closer together and give you a warm, fuzzy feeling at the same time.

- **Play a game of 1-on-1-** Again with that theme of friendly competition and exercise. Do you get the impression that these are important elements of a fun time? Most communities have public basketball courts.

- **Attend a concert-** Check out your community's concert schedule. Many will have summer concerts in the park for free.
- **Go to the museum-** Many museums have times that cost less than others, while a few will even have 'free nights.'
- **Go to a local festival-** Local festivals are a great way to have a lot of fun for a little dough.
- **Go to the drive-in-** Ah, the drive-in. How many of us are old enough to remember going to a drive-in movie? There are still some drive-in theaters out there, and nobody can stop you from bringing your refreshments from home.
- **Go to a karaoke bar-** Don't just go, participate; sing, laugh and have fun!
- **See a play-** Your local high school or college might have a production happening that you would both enjoy for a reasonable cost.
- **Bone up on your history-** Become a tourist in your hometown. Most places have historic sites nearby, and the cost is generally minimal.
- **Pizza in the park-** Pick up your favorite pie to go and make a picnic of it.
- **How sweet it is-** Eat a light dinner at home, then go to a fancy restaurant just for des-

sert. After all, who really has room for dessert after eating out?

- **Open house-** See what open houses are happening in your community. Sometimes it's nice to just look at something different and dream.
- **Go to the zoo-** Most zoos are relatively inexpensive when it's only for two.
- **The botanical gardens-** This idea works no matter what the weather. Depending on the season, you could find special exhibits such as Christmas displays.
- **Go antiquing-** Browse a few antique stores and see what unique things you find there. Sometimes it's nice just to look.
- **Fly a kite-** An inexpensive way to spend time in the park.
- **Go camping-** State parks are usually cheaper than privately owned camping facilities and have more to check out too.
- **Go fishing-** Sitting alongside a local pond for a few peaceful hours can be relaxing, not to mention, provide ingredients for your evening meal.
- **Take a drive-** A drive through the country, especially in the fall, can be quite scenic.
- **Pick your own-** Many local orchards allow you to pick your own produce.

- **Row your boat-** Rent a rowboat or canoe at your local waterway and take turns paddling along.
- **Get to know the birds-** Especially in times of heavy migration such as spring and fall, birdwatching can be fun. See who can spot the most species.
- **Geocaching-** The app is free, and who wouldn't like a treasure hunt?
- **Have a bonfire-** If you live where burn pits are allowed, an evening spent sitting around the fire is romantic. Bring back good memories as you roast hot dogs and marshmallows.
- **Go to the mall-** Remember roaming the mall as a teen? Well, you can still do that now, but instead of a pack of your peers, you'll have your significant other at your side. Window-shop to your heart's content, get a slushie, buy a warm, soft pretzel, or a giant cookie.
- **The local flea market-** There are great finds to be had for pennies. See what treasure you can find.
- **Video game marathon-** While the kids are away, the parents can act like kids again. Challenge your partner to a video game competition.

- **Have a game night**- Board games are not just for kids either. Break out the board games and snacks.
- **Movie night**- Rent, stream, or pull out some movies you haven't seen in a while. Pop some popcorn and settle in for some uninterrupted movie time.

Date-night doesn't have to break the bank. There are so many creative ideas to spend time together without spending a lot of money. We've named a few here. You could take these suggestions or come up with some of your own.

CHAPTER 9
USE COUPONS

Ah, couponing. Many of us remember waiting for the Sunday paper and the plethora of coupons that would help determine your menu for the coming week. We'd sit cross-legged on the floor with a pair of scissors surrounded by leaflets and flyers, sorting and clipping, looking for the best deals. Now, with your busy lives and the digital age, you might have foregone couponing. However, if you're trying to find ways to save money and get yourself out of debt, it may be time to bring back the coupon! Here are some steps to get you started:

- **Where to look**

    o **Sunday paper**- In our digital age, you may think that paper coupons are a thing of the past. Well, unlike the Dodo they still exist! You can still open your Sunday paper and find those flyers and inserts. It really is a rather pleasant way to spend a Sunday afternoon if you think about it as a sort of treasure hunt.

- Magazines- You can find some pretty good coupons in magazines such as Better Homes & Gardens, Woman's Day, and Good Housekeeping. Think about what types of coupons you're looking for, and that should probably steer you toward the right magazine. For example, if you're looking for coupons for makeup, you probably won't find it in Car and Driver.

- Printable coupons- There are sites dedicated specifically to coupons where they seem to gather coupons from across the board and deliver them directly to your inbox. You can also go right to the website of your favorite companies like Campbell's, Betty Crocker, Colgate, etc. to check for coupons.

- Tearpads/Blinkies- You've probably run across these at your local grocery store from time to time. Attached directly to the shelf located just below the item you're looking for, a small plastic dispenser with a blinking light to get your attention and a coupon sticking out. You tear off the coupon and presto, a new coupon scrolls out. That or a tablet-like pad of coupons with instructions for you to 'take one.'

- ○ **eCoupons-** For those of you with Smartphones (and that section of our populations seems to be growing), you may have already discovered eCoupons. You may need to download or install a certain app. When you get to the register, you present your phone to the cashier showing the correct barcode, and voila! Instant discount!

- **When can you use coupons?** Now that you know where to find your coupons, you need to know when to use them.
  - ○ **It's on sale! –** It's simple math; you can save more money if you wait until your item is already on sale, then add the savings of a coupon on top of that.
  - ○ **Sales run in cycles-** There are cycles of about 8-12 weeks for sale items. If a sale for an item just ended and you can wait, in 8-12 weeks it will probably be on sale again. There are certain things that go on sale around holidays or certain seasons as well. Remember those great sales of holiday candy the day after the holiday ends?
- **How do I use coupons? –** Does your store honor competitors' coupons? Don't know? Ask the customer service department. Here are some other ways:

- **Double coupons-** Although with the advent of the superstores and big chain discount stores this practice is slowly falling by the wayside, you should see if your store still offers this. Some stores will double your coupon up to a certain amount. A coupon worth $0.25 suddenly nets you $0.50 in savings. It may not seem like a lot, but every little bit helps.
- **Competitor coupons-** Some stores will honor coupons put out by their competitors. It never hurts to ask. Call ahead to find out before filling your cart, that way you won't be disappointed at the checkout.
- **Stacking-** While you can't use two manufacturer's coupons for the same product, some stores will let you use one of their in-store coupons in addition to a manufacturer's coupon. This practice is called stacking.
- **Stock up-** Now I'm not advocating buying so much toilet tissue that you need another room added on to your house just to hold it all. What I am saying is that when you see something that you use on a regular basis for an unbelievably good deal, buy a few extra.

If you're new to couponing, you may be a little confused by the jargon used in referring to special coupon deals. Well, worry no more! Here is your guide to understanding couponese:

- **BOGO/B1G1-** Buy 1, Get 1 free
- **BOGO 50%-** Buy 1, Get 1 50% off
- **$1/2-** $1 off 2 items
- **DND-** Do Not Double
- **UPC-** Universal Product Code (the little barcode on the package)
- **RC-** Rain Check
- **SCO-** Self Check Out
- **PSA-** Prices Start At
- **MRG/MFR-** Manufacturer coupon
- **IP-** Internet printed coupon
- **MIR-** Mail-in Rebate
- **OYNO-**On Your Next Order
- **CRT-** Cash Register Tape Coupon
- **CS-** Customer Service
- **EXP-** Expires

If you've never been one to coupon, there are some important points you need that you need to know.

- **Fake coupons-** One of the problems with internet coupons is, it may not be real, especially if it's from an unknown source. If you've found a coupon online and you're not quite sure if it's legitimate, there are some ways that you can check to make sure. Go to the website centsoff.com and check out their list of fraudulent coupons.

- **Don't Copy!** – While it might sound like a good idea, it's actually considered fraud and is against the law. So, DON'T DO IT!

- **Pay attention to how it's meant to be used-** If the coupon is for a certain size or flavor of an item, only use it for that size or flavor. Don't try to use a coupon meant for $0.50 off 13 lbs. or more of a brand of dog food for a 10 lb. bag.

- **One Per Purchase-** If a coupon says 1 per purchase, it means that you can only use one coupon per item. If it says 1 per transaction, that means that you will only be able to use 1 of those coupons per your entire trip.

Now that you've learned a little about coupons, you can start to change the way you approach shopping.

- **Start small-** You probably won't go from spending $250/week to being that lady who gets her entire shopping trip for free immediately (or at all), but you can save some significant coinage with a little practice. Start small, with just one store. Once you've mastered that, you could branch out to a few stores if that doesn't have you driving all over town and wasting the money you're saving on gas.

- **Be willing to try new things-** We are creatures of habit, and we all have our favorite brands, but if you're willing to try new brands, you could save a lot of money. Again, start small, just one or two new brands that you've found a coupon for at a time. You may find your new favorite.

- **Shop a little differently-** In the past, you may have bought only what you needed for that week. Now you're looking for bargains and sales. Stockpile (on a small scale) while the prices are low. Buy three or four boxes of your favorite cereal while it's on sale and you have a couple of BOGO coupons for instance.

Many of us spend thousands of dollars a year on groceries alone. Just like those grocery bills add up, so do the coupon savings over time. If you save just $25 a week off of your grocery bill, then by the end of the year you could be $1200 ahead by the end of the year!

Coupon Clipping Log

Coupon	Company	Date Expires	Coupon Value	Stores That Accept	Category	Note

CHAPTER 10
GAIN SOME EXTRA INCOME, AND TRY NOT TO SPEND MORE THAN YOU EARN

Believe it or not, there are tons of ways to earn a little extra money on the side. When you are trying to get out of debt, just about everything is fair game. Look at all of your assets and determine whether or not you can live without it. What is an asset? An asset is anything that you own. Your mind may automatically go to your car or your home, but don't stop there, think outside the box. What about those baseball cards resting comfortably in the shoebox in the top of your closet? Will you really miss that treadmill collecting dust and cobwebs in the corner? Most of us have more than what we really need, and some of it could be put to work for us instead of just taking up space. You may be cash poor, but asset rich.

- **Put your assets to work-** You don't have to part with an asset in order to get something out of it. Some of them can be put to work for you. You can get paid just for driving your car! Have you ever seen a car with logos covering them? It's called car wrapping. Car wrapping has actually been around almost as long as cars. Back in the 1920's businesses saw the advertising potential of covering taxis in vinyl decals. Fast forward to the present, and there are advertising companies that specialize in car wrapping. You must sign up with these agencies and give a few details about what type of car you have and what your commute is like. Once you are in their database, they will contact you when they have an ad that matches your unique profile. You will then have your car 'auto wrapped' and a vinyl decal will be placed over part or all of your car creating the illusion that it is a custom paint job advertising a certain product. You can make anywhere from $200-$1,000 a month, with the average being about $400! Imagine getting $400 a month just for doing the driving that you would be doing anyway. It's like free money!

Unfortunately, unscrupulous people have taken advantage of people trying to make legitimate money. You may have been contacted by what appears to be a legitimate car wrapping company, or maybe you saw an ad saying that you could make a few hundred dollars using their method. They then send a check for more than was originally agreed upon telling you to deposit the check, keep your share and forward the rest to a certain car wrapping company. Sadly, in a few days that check will bounce and you will be left holding the bag, responsible for the hundreds of dollars that you forwarded.

If you are asked to be the middleman between them and the car wrapping vendor, it's a scam. Period. A legitimate business would pay the vendor directly.

- **Rent a room-** If you aren't really looking to downsize your home, but you aren't currently using all of it, you may want to take in a lodger. If you've ever watched an old black and white movie or television show, you may have seen the idea of a boarding house. Barney had a room at a boarding house in *The Andy Griffith Show*, Mork rented a room from Mindy, and Mrs. Bailey ran a boarding house in *It's a Wonderful Life*. It doesn't have to include meals, just a place to live.
- **Become a tutor-** Do you have a special skill? You could give music lessons, offer IT solutions, or offer to tutor students for a small fee.
- **Start something new-** You might even consider taking up freelance writing. There are

many online sites that will pay you to write on topics of their choosing.

- **Get a part-time job-** One of the assets that people tend to overlook is their time. Even a part-time job can give you an extra $150 or more per month depending on how many hours you can get in, and it doesn't have to be permanent. Once your debts are paid off, you can leave your part-time job, or you may just decide that you enjoy having a little extra.

- **Pawn it-** Pawnbrokers are no longer considered seedy establishments. They have become downright respectable. If you're not ready to part with your belongings for good, and you think you might come up with the means to get them back in the near future, you may want to consider finding a reputable pawnbroker.

- **Sell it-** While selling an asset is your last resort, it is an option. Just like downsizing your home, you may find that selling your new car and going with an older, but reliable used one makes better financial sense. You may decide that having a bass boat sitting in your driveway that only gets used two or three times a year while you struggle to pay your bills, makes little sense. Same goes for a motorcycle or really anything that isn't an actual need in your life. Sometimes we just have to make sacrifices to reach our goals.

- **Cut back-** If you look, you'll probably find several ways that you can cut back in your spending. Go from cable to antenna television. Carpool to save gas. Brown bag it instead of eating out for lunch. Buy cheaper seats like back-row instead of the more expensive front-row seats to an event. Go to the hairdresser less often.

- **Don't live beyond your means-** This seems like common sense, but you'd be surprised at the number of people who spend more than they make. They end up 'robbing Peter to pay Paul' so to speak. Whether it's by buying things on credit or using money that should be earmarked for paying bills on things that they can do without, they're spending more than they're earning.

The bottom line is, don't underestimate your assets. Come at things with a fresh perspective. Maybe even enlist the help of a friend to evaluate what you have that may be of value to someone else.

Extra Income Notes

So, in conclusion, don't give up! You can become debt-free. It may not happen overnight, but it can happen. The ideas presented in this book are a great jumping off point for you, they are simple and easy to follow. Just stay the course. You should be able to find something that can work for you, and if you don't, there is probably something here that at least sparks an idea that can start a fire under you big enough to get you motivated. Your journey to a debt free life starts now. You can do this!

www.ingramcontent.com/pod-product-compliance
Lightning Source LLC
Chambersburg PA
CBHW032015190326
41520CB00007B/489